The Story Frog phonics pack
An early literacy course for parents/caregivers

This course has been designed by an early years specialist, qualified teacher and mum to give you and your child the best foundation required to understand the process of young children learning to read and write through phonics and early literacy skills.

The course was created in response to the feedback from parents of young children who did not feel that they had the understanding or support to feel empowered that they could themselves, introduce early literacy skills, which supported children's future learning in schools and nurseries through a phonics based approach.

Copyright © 2015 Kate Daurge, The Story Frog ®
Trademark registered UK

Not only does this course aim to encourage children and empower parents but it is also designed to give an understanding and overview of the skills and knowledge young children can acquire in preparation for entry to school, in line with expectations outlined in the Early Years Curriculum.

The story Frog course is fun, enriching and engaging and aims to celebrate individual children's achievements through play based, fun activities, which are linked to their own interests.

The course is split into three terms and each sound is introduced on a given day.

Day two is intended to follow on from day one, once a child has had long enough on the skills presented for each day it is then time to move on. It is recommended that the course is worked through at the child's own pace with a general guide being a week between "days" for younger children (2/3 years), equally though you can pick up the course no matter how much time has passed between days/sounds. For older children (4/5/6 years) this course can be used at a quicker pace and could also be used daily as a catch up for those with gaps in their phonic knowledge.
Give your child time to learn each sound and undertake the progression of key skills at their own pace to coincide

with their own developmental rate. It is better for children to have a strong foundation than to rush through learning to read, remember our approach is that we want your child to love reading and writing.

This course is designed to be delivered to children from age 2 and up, although children will gain different skills and progress at different rates depending on their age.

Most important is the time given to help your child to consolidate their learning through play and enjoyment of stories, imaginative play and exploration.

Time is dedicated throughout the course to; reading and writing skills, fine and gross motor skills, messy play, creative play and language, all of which are fundamental for your child's development and enjoyment.

The key to success is to encourage your child to persevere, challenge themselves, have a go and above all develop a love of learning and of stories through real experiences and fun, stimulating and exciting play based activities.

Whether you undertake this learning journey with your child over a year, longer or even a much shorter time, the goal is to create a strong foundation for their learning of literacy.

Enjoy the course! Have fun and help your child to sparkle!

Copyright © 2015 Kate Daurge, The Story Frog ®
Trademark registered UK

Top tips:
- Make sure you are pronouncing the sounds correctly: if you need help with the sounds visit our YouTube page and watch our sounds video just search for The Story Frog.
- Always ensure you use lower case letters to practise whether you buy magnetic or foam letters or simply when writing them yourself. A5 child's oral blending/sound cards are available purchase to support your time using this course – please go to our website to order them www.thestoryfrogphonics.com
- Make sure you read to your child every night at least one story.
- Visit the library and get your child to choose books that they are interested in.
- Never sit at the table – find a nice cozy nook in their play space or go outside!
- Give your child lots of praise –learning to read is one of the most difficult things to do.
- Your child wants to please you – show them how proud you are.
- Always go at your child's own pace working through the course at the rate that seems comfortable to them and you.
- Remember children can only concentrate for a number of minutes – as a guide use their age e.g. three years old means three minutes maximum!

Copyright © 2015 Kate Daurge, The Story Frog ®
Trademark registered UK

Copyright © 2015 Kate Daurge, The Story Frog ®
Trademark registered UK

Day 1

Look at the s page together.
Demonstrate how to make the s sound as in s in "snake", get your child to look at your mouth and the shape it makes.
Get them to say s explain that this is a long sound "ssss".

Ask, "Can you make a loud s, quiet s, angry s, and shy s?
Say "we slide down an s" and with your finger, trace the s on the s page.
Get your child to traces s on the s page.
Look at the pictures together and ask, "What can you see?"
Child says, "sand" say "yes that's right s-a-n-d - sand"

Child says "star" say "yes that's right s-t-ar star"

Child says "sock" say "yes that's right s-o-ck sock"

Child says, "snow" say "yes that's right s-n-ow snow".
Lots of praise! Tell your child how amazing they are!
Things you could do at home:
Show your child the "s" sound and get them to draw an s in different ways – in sand, glitter or shaving foam.
Make an s scrapbook and stick in things you find with an "s" sound e.g. stick, sand, star, soap etc. You can even include photos of places or things you see with an 's' in them e.g. 'station'

Copyright © 2015 Kate Daurge, The Story Frog ®
Trademark registered UK

S

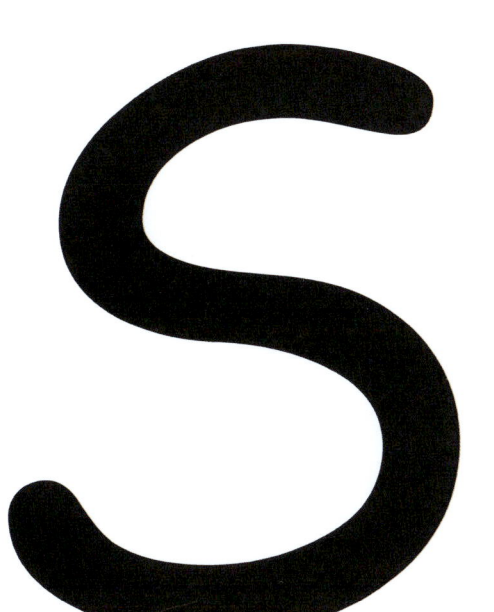

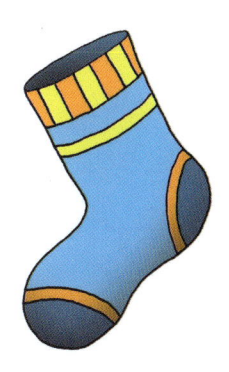

Day 2

Remind your child of the previous sound they learnt: S
Show your child the s page and ask them to remind you what sound this makes.
Tickle time - allow them to trace an s on their hand, foot, on your back etc.

Introduce new sound a.
Show your child the a sound page and say and repeat with them a as in apple.
Talk about the shape of the a – that it is round and has a tail.
Get your child to trace the a using their finger.
Look at the a page and ask, "What can you see?"

Child says, "ant" say, "yes that's right a-n-t ant".

Repeat with ankle, apple and anchor.

Lots of praise! Tell your child how amazing they are!

What you can do at home:
This week focus on letter formation: make lots of opportunities for your child to form their letter sounds in lots of different ways, use; glitter, shaving foam, paint, sand, marker pens or even the soil outside. They now have two sounds so can practise forming a and s.

Copyright © 2015 Kate Daurge, The Story Frog ®
Trademark registered UK

a

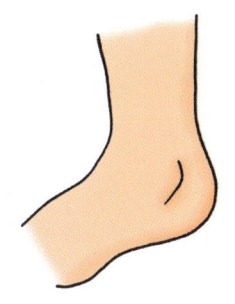

Copyright © 2015 Kate Daurge, The Story Frog ®
Trademark registered UK

Day 3

Review previous sounds: s and a.

Show your child the s and a pages and remind them of the sounds these letters make.

Write the sounds on post its and push the two sounds together to make the word "as", say the sounds slowly "a – s, a – s, a – s" until they hear the word "as" – this skill is called oral blending, remember to try to not give them the answer.

Introduce the new sound t.

Show your child the t page and say and repeat with them t as in tip (try not to say "tu" but a short sharp "t" as in "tennis"). Talk about the shape of the t – that it is tall with a line through it, you could repeat "cross the t".

Ask your child to copy and trace the t.

Look at the pictures and ask, "What can you see?"

Child says, "tap" say, "yes that's right tap t-a-p"

Repeat with tank, tent and tick.

Lots of praise! Tell your child how amazing they are!

What you can do at home:

Focus on oral blending, this is the skill to introduce hearing sounds in words and it is vital for reading. Ask your child to put there hands on their h-ea-d, their n-o-se, their n-e-ck (breaking down the sounds as you hear them in words), ask your child to fetch you a "p-e-n". Repeat this many times and in many ways and your child will start to hear the sounds in words. (Some children will already have this skill and for others it will take them much longer to hear the sounds in words and more practise is needed, both stages are normal developmentally in early childhood).

Copyright © 2015 Kate Daurge, The Story Frog ®
Trademark registered UK

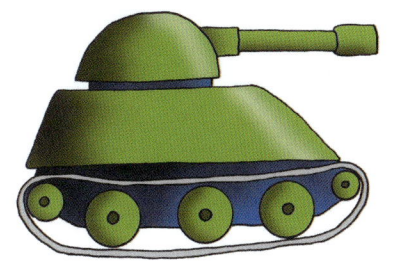

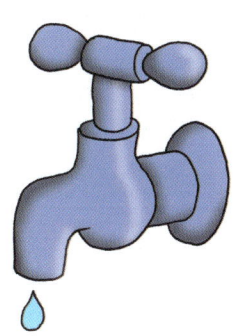

ge, The Story Frog ®

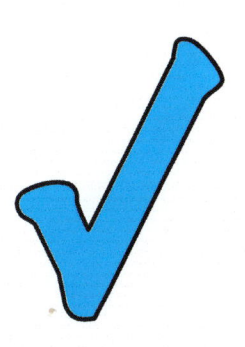

Day 4

Review previous sounds; s, a and t

Show your child the s, a and t sounds and remind them of the sounds these letters make.

Write the sounds on post its and push the three sounds together to make the word "sat" and say the sounds slowly "s-a-t, s-a-t, s-a-t," until they hear the word "sat".

Introduce new sound p.

Show your child the p page and say and repeat with them p as in pot.

Give your child a mirror to look in whilst they make this sound ask "what do you need to do with your mouth"?

Give your child a tray of glitter, can they make a p sound in it?

Use oral blending to help children find the sounds on the page, for example; "can you find a p-e-n? a p-i-n? a p-l-u-m? and a p-a-n? Be careful not to give your child the answer but allow them to hear the sounds in words instead.

Lots of praise! Tell your child how proud you are of how well they are doing.

What you can do at home:

This time, really focus on those fine motor skills, give your child lots of cutting activities, use, play dough, threading beads, using tweezers and tiny sequins. Model how to have patience and not to give up by joining in with them.

Copyright © 2015 Kate Daurge, The Story Frog ®
Trademark registered UK

p

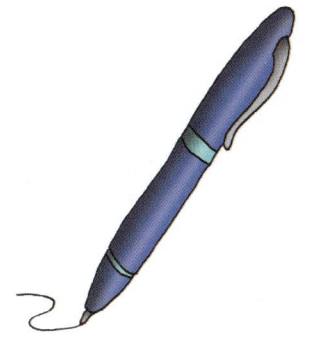

Copyright © 2015 Kate Daurge, The Story Frog ®
Trademark registered UK

Day 5

Review previous sounds; s,a,t,p

Show your child the s, a, t and p sounds and remind them of the sounds these letters make – look in the mirror and ask "what do you have to do to make each sound"?

See how many words you can make together with these sounds. Start with sat, s-a-t (see if your child can hear the sounds and put them together to make "sat") now change the s for a p, what word is it now? Repeat, finding other words.

Introduce new sound i.

Show your child the i page and say and repeat with them "i" as in "ink".

Ask your child to draw an i on their hand/ on your back/ on the wall using their finger.

Give your child a tray of shaving foam, can they make an i sound in it? Don't forget to dot your i.

Repeat the oral blending activity from last time, be careful to ensure that you really break down those words i-n-k and bring the sounds closer together as you repeat them until your child hears the word for example: "i----n---k, i—n—k, i-n-k.

Lots of praise! Give your child a high five!

What you can do at home:

This time, lets practise our gross motor skills, use big tools for digging in the garden, paint with rollers, and shoot basketball hoops. Remember to keep practicing those oral blending skills, make getting dressed into a game, ask your child, "can you find your t-o-p" etc. Always look for the sounds your child knows in the environment.

Copyright © 2015 Kate Daurge, The Story Frog ®
Trademark registered UK

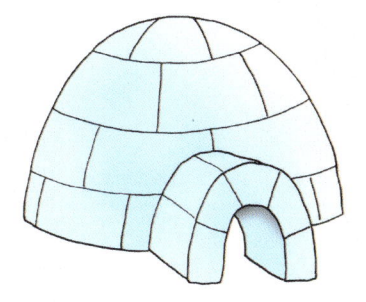

i

Day 6

Review previous sounds;
Show your child the s, a, t, p and i sounds and remind them of the sounds these letters make.
Hang your sounds on the washing line, how many words can we make on the line? Ask your child, "Can we make a word beginning with n?"
Introduce new sound n.
Show your child the n page and say and repeat with them "n as in nose". Say this is a long sound like an airplane "nnnnnnnnn"
Ask your child to trace the n with their finger
Give your child a large piece of paper and stick it on a wall outside, or inside. Can they make a n sound, give them different apparatus, large paint brushes, pens, chalks and see how many different n sounds they can make.
Look at the pictures and ask, "What can you see?"
Ask your child what each picture is of and what sounds they can hear in each word, for example "net", have a go at writing the words together, but join in and model the letters they have not yet learnt.
Lots of praise! Give your child a hug.
Well done! You have reached the end of term 1! Spend some time practicing oral blending using the sounds you have so far: s,a,t,p,i and n, find examples of these sounds and words that are in the environment around you and try and read the sounds and blend them, reading the words together. Once your child has memorized these sounds and blend the sounds together they should be able to begin tackling two and three letter words.

Copyright © 2015 Kate Daurge, The Story Frog ®
Trademark registered UK

n

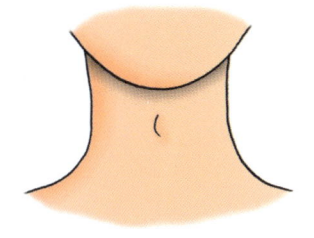

je, The Story Frog ®
Trademark registered UK

End of Term 1 ideas Sheet:

Spend some time revisiting and consolidating the sounds you have learnt this term and think about the skills that your child has mastered and those that they are still developing. Repeat the activities they loved and adapt the ones they found tricky.

Remember it is all about developing a love of learning and celebrating your child's individual achievements. Some children will master their sounds quickly but might find oral blending more difficult. For these children it is very important that you spend time listening to the sounds around you, stop them wherever you are and ask "what can you hear?"

It may feel that it is taking them a long time to blend those sounds together but don't rush, they will develop that skill, just keep going. A really good activity is to find objects that are three letters long or pictures of objects such as a pen or a pin and write the words on post it notes, get your child to match the words and objects together using their knowledge of the sounds they know and listening for the initial sounds in words.

If your child is blending well but does not seem to be retaining their sounds this is also quite typical. Don't rush, it is good to repeat sounds over and over again and use the sounds they do know to start reading words together. Some children are not ready to read at this stage in a developmental sense and that is okay too, you are setting the groundwork so that when they are ready the process will be much quicker and easier for them. When you are ready move on to term two!

Copyright © 2015 Kate Daurge, The Story Frog ®
Trademark registered UK

Copyright © 2015 Kate Daurge, The Story Frog ®
Trademark registered UK

Day 7

Review all the sounds so far: s,a,t,p,i,n
Show your child the sound page m.
Model how to make the m sound as in m in "mum".
Get them to say "m" (remember this is a long sound "mmmm" Ask, "Can you draw an m in the air?"
Say "to make an m we must go up and down up and down"
Child copies and traces m on the m page.
Ask your child to draw an m on their hand, on your back, on their knee, on teddy's hand etc.

Look at the pictures and ask, "What can you see?"
Ask the children to point to the picture you are sounding out – tell them you are going to speak as slowly as a snail to make the words e.g. m-u-m.
Blending game – give the children the words to match them with their pictures with their adult's help, write the words on post its.
Lots of praise! Tell your child how amazing they are!
Things you could do at home:
- Get your child to write the sounds that they know on the pavement outside using big chalk and draw pictures of items beginning with those sounds.
- Put pictures of short three letter words (CVC or consonant, vowel, consonant) around the room e.g. sun, bag etc. get your child to find them by reading out the words to them as above (as slowly as a snail).

Copyright © 2015 Kate Daurge, The Story Frog ®
Trademark registered UK

m

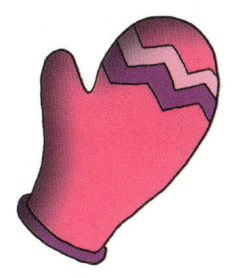

Day 8

Review all of the sounds so far:

S,a,t,p,i,n,m,

Show your child the sound page d.

Model how to make the d explaining that this is a short sound.

Get them to say "d" whilst looking in the mirror.

Ask, "Can you draw a d on your hand?"

Child copies and traces d on the d page using their finger.

Ask your child which sounds they can hear in "dog" or in "dig".

Have a go at writing more than one sound together – use a mini whiteboard or blackboard and chalk and get your child to have a go at writing d-i-p ask them what sounds they can hear. They might get the initial and last sound but can they hear that middle sound?

Lots of praise! Tell your child how fantastic they are!

Things you could do at home:

Focus on cooking skills (all good skills for developing fine motor) did you know cooking skills for the under fives include: kneading, mashing, grating, chopping and spreading. Your child will really enjoy a simple task like making sandwiches and as well as developing their fine and gross motor skills it also helps them to become more independent and "have a go" at new activities, both important skills for being ready to learn.

Copyright © 2015 Kate Daurge, The Story Frog ®
Trademark registered UK

d

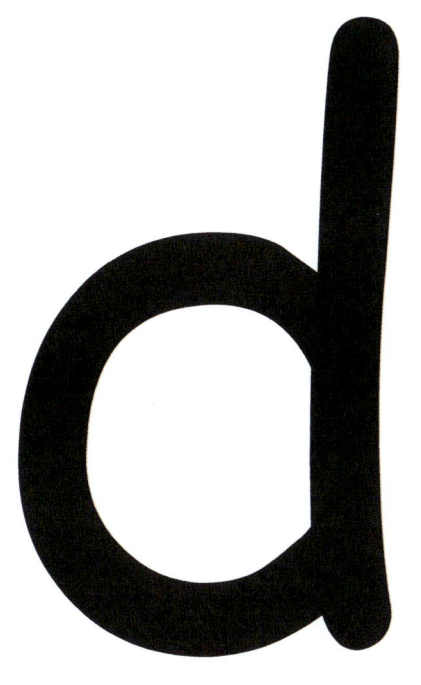

Day 9

Review all of the sounds so far:
S,a,t,p,i,n,m,d,
Show your child the sound page f.
Model how to make the f explaining that this is a long sound. Get them to say "f".
Ask, "Can you draw a f on the floor using your finger?"
Child copies and traces f on the f page.
Ask your child to show you what they can see on the page – can they segment the sound? (segment means to hear the sounds in each word).
Writing on big paper – use your sound board to have a go at writing the word on paper and forming the sound f, you could use wallpaper or wrapping paper, roll out all the paper and explore!
Lots of praise! Tell your child how brilliant they are!
Things you could do at home:
- Messy play – fill up your sand tray and get your child to find sounds they know in the tray (use "snow" if it is winter or slime, paper shreds anything sensory to explore).
- Strengthen the muscles in your little ones hands by giving them lots of opportunities to cut, stick and collage this week as well as form letters using dual control scissors or loop scissors if your child has difficulty cutting, use the rhyme, "finger on the bottom, thumb on the top open the mouth and go chop chop chop" to remember how to hold scissors.

f

Day 10

Review all of the sounds so far:

S,a,t,p,i,n,m,d,f

Show your child the c page.

Model how to make the c explaining that this is a short sound. Get them to say "c".

Ask, "Can you draw a c on your hand?"

Explain to your child that if they master drawing a c sound on paper they can use this as a basis to begin writing other letters e.g. a, d, g etc. lots of sounds start with the c shape.

Child copies and traces c on the c page.

Ask your child to show you the objects they can see which begin with a c sound.

Writing in paint – have a go at letter formation in paint! You could do this on the floor or stick your paper to the wall and stand up – have a go with fingers, paint brushes, rollers, fly swatters, or sticky tape bamboo to the end of brushes to make them extra long!

Lots of praise! Tell your child how fantastic they are!

Things you could do at home:

- Explore storybooks this week with your child, ask them to choose a story and say to them "can you show me the front cover? What does the picture tell us about the story? See if your child can open the book correctly and hold it the right way up. Can they point to the text? Ask them, "where do we start reading from?" Repeat with lots of different stories.

Copyright © 2015 Kate Daurge, The Story Frog ®
Trademark registered UK

C

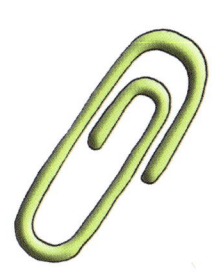

Day 11

Review all of the sounds so far:
S,a,t,p,i,n,m,d,f,c
Show your child the g sound page.
Model how to make the g explaining that this is a short sound. Get them to say "g".
Ask, "Can you make a g with play dough?"
See if they can make a g over the big g on the g page using dough.
Oral blending time again ask your child to point to the word you are sounding out "granny", "girl", "grape", "gate". Words that have an e on the end are split digraphs – g-a-m-e is actually three sounds like d-i-g, game is g-a(split e)-m. you could explain to your child that the e is helping the a in game become an "ay" sound rather than an "a" sound, without the e on the end it would read "gam". To simplify this tell your child that the e is holding hands with the a making it say its name "ay" – so three sounds altogether and not four.
Lots of praise! Tell your child how fantastic they are!
Things you could do at home:
- Retell a story this week – ask your child to pick their favourite story and tell you it all by themselves – you will be surprised by what they know and this is all great language for when they become writers.
- Get a big piece of paper and draw the story with your child – who are the characters? And what happens to them? Draw some key sounds from the story too.

g

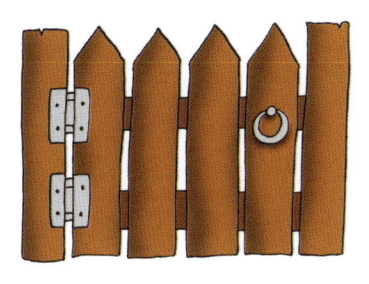

Day 12

Review all of the sounds so far:
S,a,t,p,i,n,m,d,f,c,g
Show your child the sound page o.
Model how to make the o explaining that this is a short sound.
Get them to say "o" as in "otter."
Ask your child to watch your mouth as you say the sound, say what shape do I need to make with my lips to make an o sound?
Trace the o on the o page.
Oral blending time again ask your child to point to the word you are sounding out, sound out each word from the pictures on the o page.
Make as many words as you can using the sounds you have learnt – get your child to read them by writing the sounds own on paper and bringing them together and blending the sounds, o-n for example. Now change some of the sounds try i-n and a-n. If your child can read two letter words, try those with three letters e.g. i-m-p. Repeat. If your child is not ready to read get them to match words you write down with pictures or objects, using the sounds that they know e.g. c-a-t.
Lots of praise! Tell your child how clever they are!
Things you could do at home:
This week focus on different genres, explain the difference between fiction and non-fiction, visit the library and choose a book. Showing your child they can read something they find interesting develops their love of the written word.

Copyright © 2015 Kate Daurge, The Story Frog ®
Trademark registered UK

o

Day 13

Review all of the sounds so far:
S,a,t,p,i,n,m,d,f,c,g,o
Show your child the sound page k.
Model how to make the k explaining that this is a short sound.
Get your child to say "k" as in "key" (try not to say "ku" but make it a short "k" when you model pronunciation). Explain to your child that they already know another phoneme, which makes this sound, see if they can find it (c). Trace the k on the k page.
Child copies and traces k on the page, give your child lots of practise to form this sound as it is rather a tricky one.
Oral blending time again ask your child to point to the word you are sounding out, sound out each word from the pictures on the k page.
Did you know it is really important that your child becomes familiar with lots of different fonts, ways of writing different letters (and numbers come to think of it). They will come across these different fonts in everyday life and it is so important that they are familiar with a range.
Lots of praise! Tell your child how clever they are!
Things you could do at home:
Talk about a story that your child loves, ask them why they like it, ask them how the character is feeling and how the ending could be different. See if your child can come up with some new friends for their favourite character. Can they draw a picture of them? What do they look like? Can they give them a name?

Copyright © 2015 Kate Daurge, The Story Frog ®
Trademark registered UK

k

Day 14

Review all of the sounds so far:
S,a,t,p,i,n,m,d,f,c,g,o,k
Show your child the sound e on the e page.
Model how to make the e explaining that this is a short sound.
Get them to say "e" as in "egg".
Trace the "e" on the page.
Oral blending time again ask your child to point to the word you are sounding out, sound out each word from the pictures on the child's e page.
Fill a bag with different objects, can they find which ones contain the sound e such as p-en or p-e-g. See if your child can hear the e sound in them. If your child is ready to, get them to write some or all of the words on big paper.

Lots of praise! Tell your child they are really good at finding those sounds now and have been listening really well, which is important for learning.
Things you could do at home:

Concentrate on holding scissors this week, can your child hold the scissors with their thumb on the top and learn the rhyme; "fingers on the bottom, thumb on the top, open the mouth and go chop, chop, chop". Children enjoy cutting paper, card, pasta, bread, jelly, wool, leave, sticks in fact anything, the wider range of textures the better.

Copyright © 2015 Kate Daurge, The Story Frog ®
Trademark registered UK

e

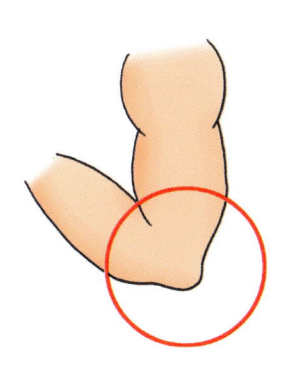

Day 15

Review all of the sounds so far
S,a,t,p,i,n,m,d,f,c,g,o,k,e
Show your child the u page.
Model how to make the u explaining that this is a short sound.
Get them to say "u" as in "umbrella"
Trace the u on the u page.

Oral blending time again ask your child to point to the word you are sounding out, sound out each word from the pictures on the u page.

Your child may begin to notice capital letters at this stage and ask what they are. It is important that your child begins to learn lower case letters only to begin with – if your child asks about a capital letter tell them what it is but still use the lower case letters predominantly at this stage.

Lots of praise! Tell your child they know so many sounds now and that's great!
Things you could do at home:

Think about rhyming this week. Can your child find words that rhyme around the home? They are some great stories with words that rhyme in them that you could read together. Help them to find words that rhyme with small words like "pop" or "tip".

Copyright © 2015 Kate Daurge, The Story Frog ®
Trademark registered UK

u

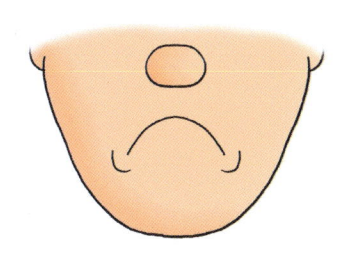

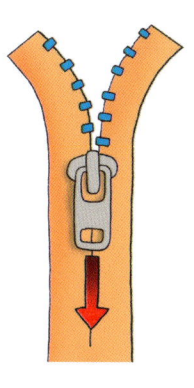

Day 16

Review all of the sounds so far:
S,a,t,p,i,n,m,d,f,c,g,o,k,e,u
Show your child the r page.
Model how to make the r explaining that this is a long sound.
Get them to say "r" (a bit like the sound a dog makes when they are growling)
Trace the r on the r page.

Oral blending time again ask your child to point to the word you are sounding out, sound out each word from the pictures on the r page.
Write down all of the sounds you have learnt on sheets of paper and lie them on the floor. Tell your child these are the stepping-stones across a river. Ask them if they can cross by landing on each sound in turn and saying the sound.

Lots of praise! If your child finds one tricky get them to copy you when saying it.
Things you could do at home:
Evaluate your child's pencil grip this week. Encourage them to hold their pen like you, holding the pen with their forefinger and thumb together and middle finger at the back. A saying might be useful for remembering this, such as "mummy and daddy in the front of the car, you in the back".

Copyright © 2015 Kate Daurge, The Story Frog ®
Trademark registered UK

r

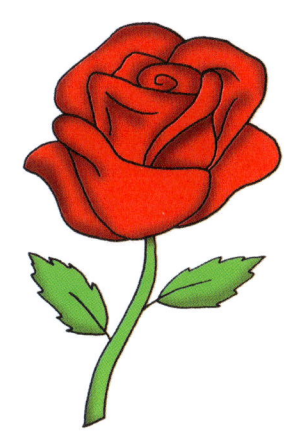

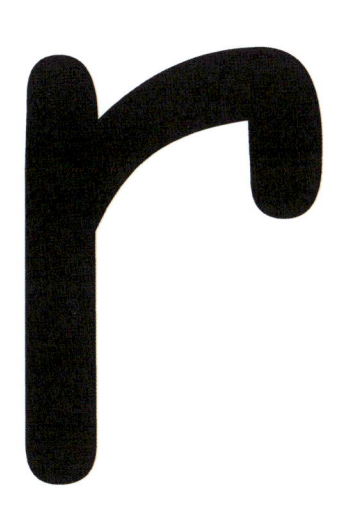

Well done you have reached the end of term two.

By now your child has been introduced to 16 sounds and a range of different activities to help them with their early reading skills.

The focus will begin to shift to writing, once your child is reading, but it is never too soon to introduce the imaginative play and story language your child will need to become a confident writer. Imagination in writing comes from real experiences and play, the most important part of a child's development.

Make sure your child has enough time to play and that you model to them how to play with a range of different toys. If your child is not keen to try new things, encourage them when you are together and let them know that if something is challenging it is good to keep trying. Show them that you also get things wrong and that's good because it means you are learning. Helping your child to become independent by dressing themselves, making their drink, brushing their own teeth, tying shoelaces, tidying up and making as many decisions as they can will help your child to gain confidence and become a more effective learner in school when the time comes (if they are not already there).

Copyright © 2015 Kate Daurge, The Story Frog ®
Trademark registered UK

Day 17

Review all of the sounds so far
S,a,t,p,i,n,m,d,f,c,g,o,k,e,u,r
Show your child the j page.
Model how to make the j as in "joke".
Get them to say "j".
Trace the j on the j page.
Oral blending time again ask your child to point to the word you are sounding out, sound out each word from the pictures on the j page.
Time for a bit of target practise – see if your child can throw a ball at the sounds that they know or shoot the sounds with a water pistol once they know the sound.
Take away any sounds they didn't remember and review them, make words with them and have a go at writing them on paper.
Lots of praise!
Things you could do at home:

Make a writing den for your child – it may be the underside of a table at home with paper stuck to the underneath, it may be a den or a tent. Make a special place where your child can go and find their sounds, write words and read stories. Fill it with some of child's favourite things and lots of different opportunities to mark make each week.

Copyright © 2015 Kate Daurge, The Story Frog ®
Trademark registered UK

j

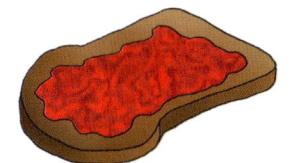

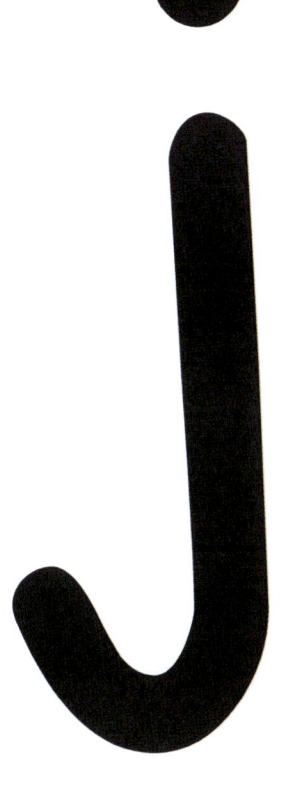

Day 18

Review: S,a,t,p,i,n,m,d,f,c,g,o,k,e,u,r,j
Show your child the h page.
Model how to make the "h" as in "hat"
Get them to say "h".
Trace the h on the h page.

Oral blending time again ask your child to point to the word you are sounding out, sound out each word from the pictures on the h page.

Take a big sock and fill it with small objects beginning with the sounds your child has learnt. Get them to put their hand in the sock and guess the items one by one by feeling them – get them to use lots of descriptive language for their guesses (e.g. how does it feel? Sharp? Soft? Slimy? Etc.). Ask your child if they know what each objects is and if they can match it to one of their sounds. Put that object with its corresponding sound and repeat.

Lots of praise!
Things you could do at home:
What is your child interested in? Decorate a box with their favourite character; whether it is Alice in Wonderland or Spiderman. They can fill this box with all their favourite writing materials and place it in their den. Refresh the boxes contents often to encourage them to mark make.

Copyright © 2015 Kate Daurge, The Story Frog ®
Trademark registered UK

h

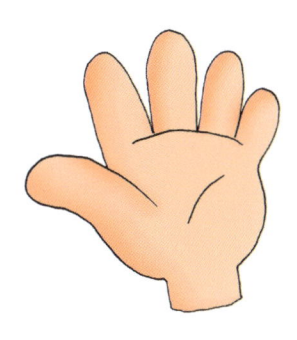

Day 19

Review: S,a,t,p,i,n,m,d,f,c,g,o,k,e,u,r,j,h

Show your child the b page.

Model how to make the b as in "bat"

Get them to say "b".

Trace the b on the b page.

Moving on from oral blending – if your child is happy to orally blend then you can give them the words on post its and get them to read them – ask them to match the words to the pictures one by one (words with more complex sounds are trickier and a child may need to look at the pictures for help – that is okay too).

This week explain to your child that there are some words that we cannot sound out and we are going to find some around the room – hide some cards around the room with the following tricky words: I, the, we, she, me, be, said etc.

See how many your child can find and bring back to you.

Explain that when reading stories this week we will see if we can find these words in the stories.

Tell them they have done well today and that the activity was really tricky.

Things you could do at home:

Get your toolbox out and let your child explore, using all the real tools with supervision. Hammering small nails or using a screwdriver really develops fine motor muscles as well as helping children to concentrate and persevere.

Copyright © 2015 Kate Daurge, The Story Frog ®
Trademark registered UK

b

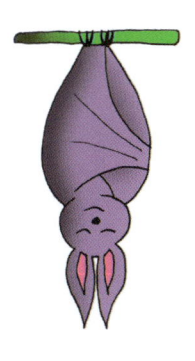

Day 20

Review: S,a,t,p,i,n,m,d,f,c,g,o,k,e,u,r,j,h, b

Show your child the l page.

Model how to make the l.

Get them to say "l".

Trace the l on the l page.

Oral blending practise/reading words as you did for day 19. Segmenting – segmenting means breaking down the words for writing – read a CVC (consonant, vowel, consonant) word normally to your child, such as l-i-t and ask them what sounds they can hear. Ask them to write down the first sound, using the soundboard to help them. Can they write the middle and final sound? Concentrate on three letter words and slowly introduce four letter (a.k.a CCVC or consonant consonant vowel consonant words) when appropriate such as "flip" etc.

Talk to your child about how far they have come and have a look at something they have done with their writing – display as much as you can and get your child to put their work up around the house to celebrate their achievements , whether it is mark making or a model they have made from dough.

Things you could do at home:

Use clay to make characters from your child's favourite story or make your own salt dough and decorate their finished model using felt tip pens.

Ask your child to tell you what their characters would say if they were here.

Copyright © 2015 Kate Daurge, The Story Frog ®
Trademark registered UK

l

Day 21

Review: s,a,t,p,i,n,m,d,f,c,g,o,k,e,u,r,j,h, b,l

Show your child the v page.

Model how to make the v.

Get them to say "v."

Trace the v on the v page.

Oral blending practise/reading words as before.

Reading challenge – challenge your child to read words appropriate to them using the sounds they have learnt on post its - make as many two, three and (if appropriate) four letter words as you can and read them together or if your child is ready they can read them independently. Once your child can read two or three words on their own celebrate and tell them they can read! You can take your child to the library and get them an early reading book – one with two or three letter words in (but not too many).

If your child is not yet ready that is normal too and there is no rush!

Things you could do at home:

Read your library book.

Buy a poster with sounds on (lower case only) and place this in your child's room – see which sounds they can recognize from it. Remember to display sounds where your child does writing as they can use this to help them to form letters.

v

Copyright © 2015 Kate Daurge, The Story Frog ®
Trademark registered UK

Day 22

Review: S,a,t,p,i,n,m,d,f,c,g,o,k,e,u,r,j,h, b,l,v

Show your child the w page.

Model how to make the w.

Get them to say "w".

Trace the w on the w page.

Oral blending practise/reading words as above

Play, play and more play – go back to basics put sounds in the sand or the soil outside and explore, find sounds and identify them, use sounds in paint, get messy and have fun.

It is really important that children learn through play and that your child enjoys the experience of learning early sounds, take your time, tailor sessions with them to their interests and ensure that they have lots of time to consolidate what they know in their play.

Things you could do at home:

Fill a tray with ice and give your child some tweezers or salad tongs, can they move the ice from one tray to another?

Give your child a bouncy ball – medium sized, can they walk from one end of the garden to the other with the ball but without using their hands to hold it?

Get your child to sit on the floor with their legs straight out in front of them and together, sat up. Tell them they need to stand up but they are not allowed to bend their legs. Can they problem solve? Join in, can you?

Copyright © 2015 Kate Daurge, The Story Frog ®
Trademark registered UK

w

Day 23

Review sounds: S,a,t,p,i,n,m,d,f,c,g,o,k,e,u,r,j,h, b,l,v, w
Show your child the qu page.
Model how to make the qu.
Get them to say "qu".
Trace the qu on the qu page.

Mark making practise – child practises making qu using small objects like cheerios or raisins to form letters.

Oral blending practise/reading words as before.
Did you know that each time you make a new sound your mouth changes shape? So if you need to know how many sounds are in the word "chap" there are three sounds, ch-a-p. Get your child to focus on your mouth when making words and ask them how many times your mouth changes shape and therefore how many sounds there are e.g. "queen" – qu-ee-n.
Things you could do at home:
Focus on learning outdoors this week:
Freeze small figures in balloons – your child's favourites and give them a small hammer and a set of golf tees, can they get them out?
Can they:
 Hammer golf tees into a melon?
Write on stones?
Write with feathers?

qu

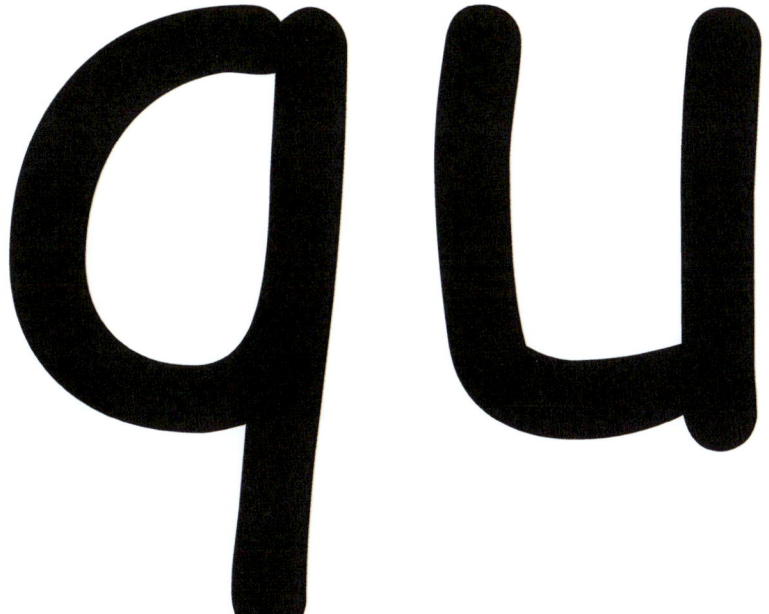

Day 24

Review: S,a,t,p,i,n,m,d,f,c,g,o,k,e,u,r,j,h, b,l,v,w,qu

Show your child the x page.

Model how to make the x.

Get them to say "x" (this is a tricky sound to make imagine you are making the x sound as it appears in the word box b-o-x).

Trace the x on the x page.

Oral blending practise/reading words as normal.

Give your child a big piece of paper and get them to lie down on it – tell them we are going to draw round them like an x ray.

Get your child to label themselves – they can have a go at the initial sound or the whole word depending on their ability level at this stage so for example they might try and write the words bones, nose, tummy etc. on their picture.

Things to do at home:

Give your child a camera and go on an adventure get them to take pictures of what they see, hear, smell and touch and then print them off and make a mini photo album for them to keep.

x

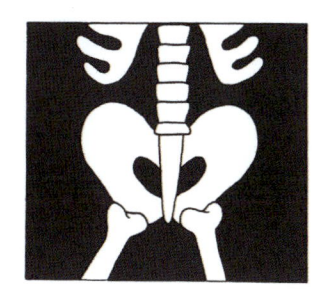

Day 25

Review: S,a,t,p,i,n,m,d,f,c,g,o,k,e,u,r,j,h, b,l,v,w,qu,x

Show your child the y page.

Model how to make the y.

Get them to say "y".

Trace the y on the y page.

Segmenting focus – show the children the picture of the child yelling on the y page. Ask can you yell? Yes I can yell. Let us see if we can remember that sentence "I can yell". Lets see if we can write it!

Explain to your child that I is a tricky word that cannot be sounded out phonetically. Get them to draw an I.

Demonstrate how to use their finger to make a finger space now ask them to segment the word "can" what sounds can they hear in "can", say "that's right c-a-n can". Finish the sentence by getting them to write the word yell (they will write it with one l sound but that is okay they are making a phonetically plausible attempt at a word and it is better not to overcorrect them at this stage (they don't yet know that a double ll can also make an l sound).

Get them to focus on what they can do this week and see how many phrases they can write e.g. I can swim /I can dance etc. Resist the urge to overcorrect them and focus on building their confidence and being full of praise!

Copyright © 2015 Kate Daurge, The Story Frog ®
Trademark registered UK

y

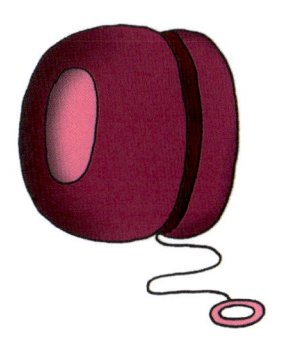

Day 26

Review: S,a,t,p,i,n,m,d,f,c,g,o,k,e,u,r,j,h, b,l,v,w,qu,x,y

Show your child the z page.

Model how to make the z as in "zoo".

Get them to say "z".

Trace the z on the z page.

Oral blending practise/reading words as normal.

Work at your child's own level with these sounds and use the activity ideas we have already touched on. As well as some of the fun ones below:

Fill a storytelling tin with items from your child's favourite stories.

Write a message in a bottle.

Bury a message underground.

Post a letter to the queen.

Write a shopping list.

Make a cardboard box into an airplane and label it.

Attach marker pens to your child's favourite cars and drive them around on big paper.

Cut up foliage.

Wash and hang up clothes.

Wash cars and hang them up make paperclip chains.

Make cup towers.

Go on a moonwalk – tie bubble wrap around your child's feet and get them to stand in paint and walk across big paper!

Copyright © 2015 Kate Daurge, The Story Frog ®
Trademark registered UK

z

Day 27

S,a,t,p,i,n,m,d,f,c,g,o,k,e,u,r,j,h, b,l,v,w,qu,x,y,z

Put the s and h sounds together and tell them that these two sounds can be combined to make the sound "sh".

Tell your child that although this is two letters it is actually one sound (this is called a digraph).
Look at the sh page and see if they can read the words. Get them to blend the sounds together.

Roll out a large piece of paper and make a list of words containing the sound "sh"
      Shop, Ship, Shack, Dish, Fish

Choose one of your words and see if your child can write a short phrase using this word.
A big ship
A pink fish

This week's activity:
Tell your child you are going to the shop and you need to make a list of things they would like to buy – they can draw the objects from their list and have a go at writing the first sound for each picture or the whole words if they are feeling adventurous.
Give your child a big hug!! Tell them how far they have come!

sh

shop

shack

dish

ship

Day 28

Review: S,a,t,p,i,n,m,d,f,c,g,o,k,e,u,r,j,h, b,l,v,w,qu,x,y,z,sh

Put the c and h sounds together and tell them that these two sounds can be combined to make the sound "ch".

Tell your child that although this is two letters it is actually one sound.

Look at the ch page and see if they can read the words. Get them to blend the sounds together.

Say some "ch" words out loud and get your child to write them down using the sound board to help them.

Choose one of your words and see if your child can write a short phrase using this word. This time emphasize finger spaces between words if you can.

    A chip shop

    A slim chap

This week's activity:

Ask your child what they love most and could they draw a picture for you this could be a dinosaur, a favourite character from a book or TV programme or an activity. Ask them what is in their picture. What is happening – can they tell you the story of their picture?

Copyright © 2015 Kate Daurge, The Story Frog ®
Trademark registered UK

ch

chap

chick

chip

chink

Day 29

Review: S,a,t,p,i,n,m,d,f,c,g,o,k,e,u,r,j,h,b,l,v,w,qu,x,y,z,sh,ch

Show your child the f sound on a post it and introduce them to the th page.

Explain that these are two different sounds and we must not get them muddled up. F is the sound of a balloon deflating and is a long sound – hold out your hands and push them together slowly as if deflating a balloon whilst making the f sound.

Now demonstrate th – put your tongue between your teeth to make this sound.

See if your child can have a go at the more complex sounds on the th page; think, thing, path, bath.

Tell your child that although this is two letters it is actually one sound.

This week's activity:

Listen to your child, ask them what they enjoy most when they are learning their sounds – target their strengths and challenge them where you can. Think about the bigger picture, is your child one that has a go at tricky activities? Do they need support to have a go? Are they confident? Do they enjoy mark making? What is their concentration like? Sit with your child and observe them, think about how they learn and what they like best.

Well done! You have come to the end of The Story Frog Course!

Copyright © 2015 Kate Daurge, The Story Frog ®
Trademark registered UK

th

thing

think

path

bath

The Story Frog

By now your child has been introduced to the initial sounds for reading and writing and will have either memorized some or all of them, or have been familiarized with them and may only remember one or two.

All children develop and learn at different rates and some are ready to learn these sounds and skills earlier than others. Every child works at their own pace and needs time to consolidate what they know through play. Did you know that playing is the most effective way for young children to learn? This course has been designed to help you, the parent, teacher or caregiver, provide the child with the necessary opportunities to learn early sounds and literacy skills.

Copyright © 2015 Kate Daurge, The Story Frog ®
Trademark registered UK

You may find you spend time revisiting many areas of this course over and over again and that is expected.

What is clear is that when children begin school having been introduced to these sounds and the associated skills, they have a far greater chance of reaching and exceeding their potential in reading as they work their way through school.

Most importantly children are far more likely to love reading, writing and stories and excel as readers and writers if they have had positive early experiences of literacy. Above all relax, go at your own pace, have fun and play with your child. Learning to read and write is one of the most challenging processes we ever go through and it is important to have fun and enjoy it.

For further support and advice please visit our website:

www.thestoryfrogphonics.com

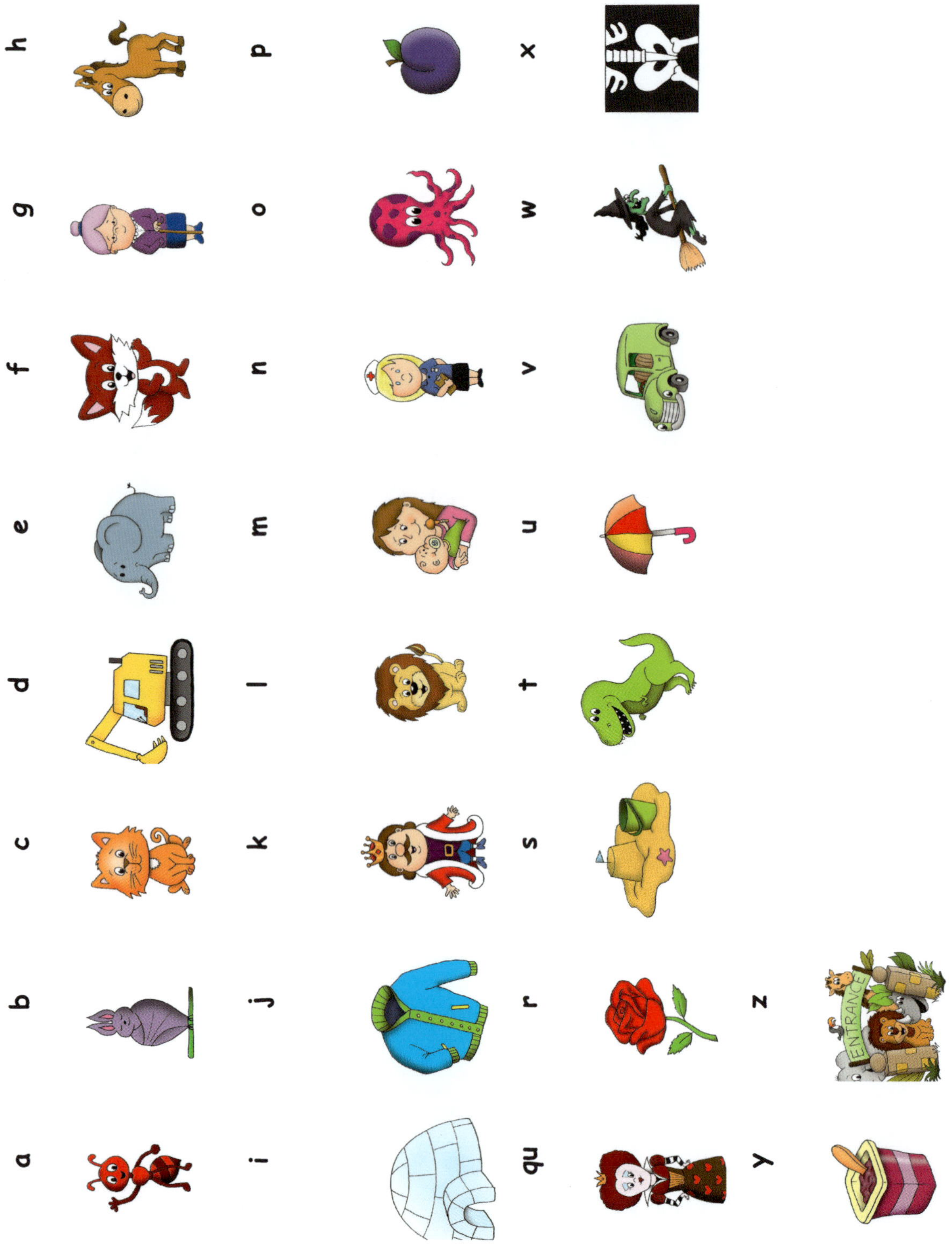
a b c d e f g h
i j k l m n o p
qu r s t u v w x
y z

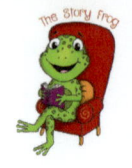

Copyright © 2015 Kate Daurge, The Story Frog ®
Trademark registered UK

First tricky words:
I
no
the
to
go
into
he
she
we
me
be
you
are
her
was
all
they
my
said
have
like
so
do
some
come
little
one
were
there
what
when
out
oh
Mrs
people
their

Printed in Great
Britain
by Amazon